FLY RODDING FOR BASS

Books by Charles F. Waterman

The Hunter's World (1970)

The Fisherman's World (1971)

Hunting Upland Birds (1972)

Modern Fresh and Salt Water Fly Fishing (1972)

Hunting in America (1973)

The Part I Remember (1974)

Fishing in America (1975)

The Practical Book of Trout Fishing (1977)

The Treasury of Sporting Guns (1979)

A History of Angling (1981)

Ridge Runners and Swamp Rats (1983)

Mist on the River (1986)

Gun Dogs and Bird Guns (1988)

Times and Places, Home and Away (1988)

Fly-Rodding for Bass (1989)

FLY RODDING
FOR BASS

Charles F. Waterman

LYONS & BURFORD, PUBLISHERS

THE CORTLAND LIBRARY

This fine book is one of a continuing series, sponsored by Cortland Line Company, Inc., Cortland, New York, designed for all fly fishermen—from beginning to advanced sportsmen. The series currently includes *Fly Rodding for Bass* by Charles F. Waterman, *Superior Flies* by Leonard M. Wright, Jr., *Practical Salt Water Fly Fishing* by Mark Sosin, and *Wade a Little Deeper, Dear: A Woman's Guide to Fly Fishing* by Gwen Cooper and Evelyn Haas.

Printed in the United States of America

10 9 8 7 6 5 4 3

Library of Congress Cataloging-in-Publication Data

Waterman, Charles F.
  Fly rodding for bass.
  (Cortland library)
  Includes bibliographical references.
  1. Bass fishing. 2. Fly fishing. I. Title.
II. Series.
SH681.W38   1989   799.1'758   89-12153
ISBN 1-55821-044-X

Contents

Introduction

B lack bass rose to flies long before baitcasting reels had level wind, and certainly long before monofilament began to swish from spinning reels. All of this time there have been fly fishermen for bass, although the first bass flies I saw were gigantic copies of wet trout patterns.

There is no doubt the black bass is America's best-known fish and that it has spread from very limited range to all of the United States except winter-chilled Alaska (I have long suspected there is a bass living somewhere in Alaska, but have no proof). Behaviorists have sagely pronounced the bass more intelligent than the trouts and bass prosper where trout disappear. Ruined trout water has been taken over by bass and the bass does a pretty good job of taking care of itself.

Fly casters may spread their talents from bass fishing but they do not outgrow it or graduate from it, and many who have caught the most finicky trout and the largest salt-water specimens regularly come back to bass. Bass and their near relatives are good to start with but they are good to finish with, too. It is easy to catch some bass on flies but last spring I stood in three feet of largemouth water, looked for a good casting spot between eelgrass beds, and contemplated a fisherman named Charlie Wiles a few yards away. Like me, he was using a bass bug as he has for many years, and it is an allegedly simple method. I saw nothing unusual about his operation but he has almost invariably caught twice as many bass as anyone else on those waters, and they are bigger fish. He guards no secrets; his skill is somewhere in his subconscious, a product of intelligent experience.

I began fly-rodding for bass on hot summer evenings on Kan-

1

sas tank ponds when thunderheads piled high and thousands of crows went home to roost. The bullbats would be busy and I waded wet on a soft bottom. Where the water was deepest, fly casters rode big inner tubes with homemade harnesses—the "belly boat" or "tube boat," which has been invented from time to time since then and greatly modernized.

The largemouths would take the bugs with startling blasts, with great bulges and gurgles—and sometimes with a delicate sucking sound—and then they would run for lily pads or dive for bottom growth; and when the short, heavy gut leader tightened they might jump with a deliberate, head-wagging, slow-motion, straight-up start, the violent shake and splattering fall-back, and a nearby heron might croak with surprise and fly away.

It was much later and far from Kansas that bass came from the tops of freshly drowned pines in California's brand-new Lake Shasta to slash a hair bug where a game trail ended at the lake's new edge. It was much later that the smallmouth bass came up from granite boulders in Maine lakes—dark shadows far down in clear water—growing larger fast and breaking out with a shallow-running streamer. And Ozark bass materialized in gliding chunk-rock water in rivers later to be dammed.

There are more bass now than ever. Admittedly, they are hard to come by with flies in some of the big impoundments—but they who say the plastic worm and the bass tournament have replaced fly fishing have moved in restricted circles, and it is a little strange to read a fat volume that purports to be a definitive treatise on all bass fishing and does not mention the fly at all. Those with the long rods are torn between an urge to praise their sport and a desire to keep it a happy secret.

There's little doubt that bass fishing began when trout anglers in the New World began to accept the fish as a strange but exciting prey. They evidently used trout flies for the new target and then tied them bigger to suit the largemouth's taste. While baitcasters adapted some of the European artificial minnows to bass fishing, there really wasn't much in the trout arsenal to match the bass bug.

Southern bass angler wades eelgrass flat.

3

Among the bass bugs of the 1930s were the Dragon Fly, Hair Mouse, and Stunted Skunk. The reel is a Zwarg, successor to the vom Hofe.

That came along pretty late in the game.

It was around 1910 or 1911 when the bass bug got its start with Ernest H. Peckinpaugh of Chattanooga, Tennessee, and fly-rodding for bass has never been quite the same since then. He had made some successful bugs for panfish and simply enlarged them for bass.

The bass had covered much of the country long before that, going west with the railroads from a rather limited range. Over the rails, tanks and buckets of tiny bass could be carried for long distances and today it's likely there are very few places where they could survive and are not present. Some of man's works destroyed the homes of millions of trout, but impoundments and warmed trout streams were accepted happily by bass.

Bass and panfish may be the best beginning for a fly fisher but the development is endless and for those who have covered a world-wide variety of fish and places it may be the most satisfying of all.

If I could have only one fish to fish for . . .

I will not finish that sentence but I could do much worse than settle down with bass. The bass is not a substitute.

What You Need

F ine tackle is one of the joys of any kind of fly fishing and most veterans have more than they really need. There's room for disagreement but there are basic needs.

The rod and line are the basis of fly fishing, and the rod is likely to be the most expensive item on the list. There are good rods at modest prices but penny-pinching should be relegated to other items. Poor rods with unmatched lines have driven beginners away and have caused fairly experienced fly casters to take up something else. Unfortunately, the beginner is least likely to have ideal equipment.

Fly rods for bass can be called middleweights, much heavier than those used with tiny flies for the most selective trout and much lighter than those used for large salt-water fish. A typical bass rod is a compromise that can be used for almost anything, a bit light for big tarpon and a bit overpowering for small trout or panfish—but usable.

Rods and matching lines have been greatly simplified by the numbering system now used by manufacturers. That is, a #8 rod (probably the most popular bass weight) should work well with a #8 line. However, I have one #8 rod that is happiest with a #10 line, and I have one #8 rod that handles a #6 line well. This is old stuff to long-time fly fishermen but can be a bit scary for a beginner. It isn't quite as complicated as it sounds. The rod and line should fit the fisherman as well as each other.

A very heavy line for a given rod is *not* a distance line and is at its best in short casts, simply because it makes the rod work with only a short section out. "Overloading" modern rods is not likely to harm them.

Heavy lines with suitable rods are best for "turning over" bulky or heavy flies or bugs. In bass fishing, rod power is needed more for casting the big lures than for playing the fish.

Fine fly rods have been made for a long time and good bass fly rods have been made for some seventy-five years. Old fly rods should be thoroughly tested before purchase, even the glass ones. There was a long period of crackpot rod manufacture—countless builders trying for something magic in extra-tippy rods, fully parabolic rods, very short rods, and very long rods. Having innocently tried all of these things, I have pretty well settled on rods that aren't unusual—except that they cast well. Frankly, it's rather hard to buy a bad new rod today, and some modestly priced moderns would have been considered marvels fifty years ago.

Like most ancients, I began fly fishing for bass with bamboo rods and some of them were quite good, in spite of being pretty heavy. Today, an eight-ounce fly rod is likely to be intended for offshore salt-water fishing. Modern glass, graphite, and boron are simply too efficient for comparison with bamboo in bass weight. Oh, some of the finest of today's fly rods are bamboo, but usually much lighter than needed for bass. Modern cane-rod makers are generally thinking of trout.

Glass is older than graphite and boron as rod material but it has not necessarily been replaced by them. However, I'll go so far as to say that 90 percent of the experienced bass fishermen I know are now using graphite or closely related material.

I was involved in a seminar for brand-new fly fishermen and various rod materials were used for teaching. When asked what rods they liked, beginners invariably chose graphite or boron, a pretty sure indication that these materials are easiest to cast with.

Bass rods must be especially tough for several reasons. First, the big wind-resistant streamers and bugs demand strength and power. Just as important is the necessity for frequently yanking bass bugs and streamers from hangups in grass or weeds. And then, while bass are seldom long runners and not as powerful as many other fish, they frequently must be held out of cover, ranging from old boat docks to lily pads. A mere tight line may not do the job.

I'm convinced that the most efficient length for bass rods is from 8 feet to 9½ feet. About 8½ feet is good but I can't tell you at the moment the exact length of any of the bundle of rods I use for bass. If the rod suits in other respects, don't worry about an inch or two of length. I have used them from 10½ feet to 6½ feet and some of the extremes were pretty good, but I seem to come back to the medium-length ones. There's nothing occult involved.

Although the "typical" bass rod is about a #8 there are special cases. For example, many of the smallmouth rivers do not demand particularly large flies and have few obstacles for a fish to dig into. The same goes for some smallmouth lakes and I've had a picnic in Maine with a #6 rod and medium-sized streamers or hair bugs. On the other end of the report is Lake Okeechobee, Florida, where I have fished big bugs in heavy pepper grass and other foliage and have used a #12 tarpon rod. A good #8 would have worked in all of these places. The #12 caused me to throw some surprised nine-inchers over my shoulder.

I knew a deep-wading lake fisherman for largemouth bass who insisted on using a bamboo trout rod that took a #4 line. He threw big bugs like a shot-putter and he kept breaking his pride and joy on both bass and hangups, but if that's what he liked, more power to him. Fly fishermen tend to collect rods for special purposes or imaginary needs, but no bass is too big or too small for a #8 rod. It will serve for panfish and will handle a northern pike as well as being at home on steelhead rivers and inshore salt water. If the action fits the caster, or if the caster adapts easily to it, further shopping is not necessary. I never said shopping wouldn't be fun.

Glass, graphite, and boron rods require little care and the later models give few ferrule problems. Unless it's to be packed in minimal space, the two-piece rod is most practical. Most of the better-class rods have cork handles but a few have good grips made of synthetics.

The grip should be full enough to give a comfortable hold when the rod is working. The very slender grip can get tiresome as a day wears on and you keep casting a powerful rod. Most rod handles are machine-turned and they do not have finger grips or a thumb rest. A rod specially shaped to fit an individual hand (possi-

Heavy-duty salt-water rod is used for largemouth bass in weedy water with large popping bug.

bly with some finger notches) is likely to be very comfortable but such a handle makes it awkward to shift a grip when your hand is tired. A few custom rods have "hammer handles," cut in an oval.

There are some casters who look good while doing it but wear blisters on their palms. Although a rather full grip should prevent excessive palm slippage, there is enough difference with individual casters that only time will tell how that works out. A large share of fly casters have a good-sized callus on their palms near the wrist.

While the "fly-caster's callus" may be worn with pride, there may be something wrong if it becomes sore with regularity, and there's certainly something wrong if a blister forms after a moderate day's casting. Of course, a light glove will save the sensitive palm but it shouldn't be necessary. If the palm gets sore it's probably a matter of gripping the rod too tightly or the exact opposite—letting it rock excessively in the palm. A very heavy rod is harder on the hand, of course, and must be offset by some extra reel weight. I carried a caster's callus for years, and then it disappeared, even though I was casting as much as ever. I don't know what changed, but the individual should keep this business in mind if he or she suffers any palm soreness.

It's the line that makes the rod work, but there is much more to it than weight. Lines are not as much fun to collect as rods but most of us could add variety to our fishing and increase our catches if we used several different ones. Having gone through years of nursing the old silk lines—dressing, drying, and coddling them—I view the modern ones with awe and appreciation. Good lines have hard finishes and enough stiffness that they do not sag much between guides.

I've said that if you have used only one line on your rod you aren't really trying. The line business is full of flat statements, often reached with little study and less experience. There are correct lines for all usable rods, but many fishermen never get around to finding them.

Of course the floating line is used more than any other and should match the rod as to weight—that doesn't necessarily mean the manufacturer's stated weights are sure to be best for you. For example, I frequently like a line that's one weight heavier than the rod calls for. Bear with me on this. I didn't say that the recommended line wouldn't work; simply that a slightly heavier or lighter line will work better in *some* cases for *some* casters. And perhaps the beginner should stick with the recommended numbers until he has his casting style well developed.

A "level" line is the same diameter for its entire length. Thousands of fly fishermen have started with it and many spent their careers with it. A "double taper" tapers down small at both ends, the purpose being to deliver the fly with delicacy, and it can be reversed on the reel if one end shows wear and tear. It, like the level line, is not intended for distance casting. It is seldom used for bass fishing although it runs well with small flies for either bass or panfish. I have used it on smallmouth streams and find it hard to beat when working very small bugs or flies for bluegills. Using it, you're less likely to slap a fly down too hard with a slightly out-of-time cast.

The "bass taper" and the "salt-water taper" are most frequently used by veteran bass fishermen for surface bugs and near-surface streamers. Their profile is a short section of small-diameter line at the leader end, a short, heavy section back of that, and a long section of smaller "running" line. The heavy part near the front will "turn over" a bulky or heavy fly or lure, causing the leader to straighten. This is a fine line but it is slightly misunderstood. It is not made for extreme distance, even though you can throw about as far with it as any bass fisherman will ever need to cast. If you carry too much of it in false casting, the small part will tend to sag. A brief casting session with this in mind will reveal more than would a hundred pages of explanation.

For extreme distance you'll go farther with the "rocket taper," which has a much longer heavy part up front. This means you can false cast much more line without its folding up on you. And here is some business that many fishermen never quite understand: the rocket taper is fine for long distance but the first few feet of a rocket taper will not be as heavy as the same length of a "bass taper." This means it will not be as convenient for short casts because the "head" or heavy part won't be off the reel. Thus there is no really perfect profile for all fishing. We have to compromise some but you should at least know why a certain line has limitations and what they are.

The bass taper is also known as a "bug taper" and the rocket taper is often called a "torpedo taper." Manufacturers describe similar profiles in different ways.

The sinking-tip line helps deep-running streamers or nymphs. That's a line with some of the forward part (generally about ten feet) made to sink instead of float and it can be had in various densities, ranging from slow to very fast sinkers. There are complete lines that sink, also in varying densities; these are usually not quite so easy to work with as the sink-tips. When really long casts are needed, the "shooting head" (usually a section of sinking line) is fastened to a very light running line, generally monofilament or very small level fly line. We'll discuss it for special situations.

Modern fly leaders, invariably monofilament, are wonders to those who were brought up on gut material. For most bass fishing long leaders aren't necessary, but there are fish in shallow, clear water that demand ten-footers, possibly tapered to three or four-pound test. There are times for delicacy and small flies always work better on light leaders. At the other extreme, a foot of heavy "shock tippet" is needed for toothy pike or pickerel. For most largemouth bass fishing, long leaders are unnecessary. About eight feet is a pretty good compromise if the fish are not leader shy and most bass fishing can be done with a leader test of eight or ten pounds. But keep an open mind on leaders. Bass can be persnickety.

Tapered leaders with spliced sections are a help in the more delicate casting, of course, a heavy butt section helping to turn over the fly; and you'll cast better if the leader isn't too limp, a little stiffness aiding as it begins to straighten out just before the fly strikes the water (to simplify things, we'll say "fly" although we include streamers, nymphs, and bugs—sometimes even small spinners).

You don't need a wide variety of knots for bass fishing—just an attachment for your fly, a connection for leader to line, one for line to backing and a splice for tapered leader sections. The nail knot and its variations are fine for line to leader, an improved clinch knot or uni-knot is good for the hook eye, and the blood knot handles sectional leader tapers and line-to-backing.

The most popular reel for bass fishing is single action and it needn't be one of the most expensive models. A multiplying fly reel has merit when you need to get loose line collected in a hurry. The automatic is fine for some spots when you don't want extra line catching in brush or large feet, but it will not handle long-running fish that you might run into. The reel needs some weight to help balance a #8 rod. In theory, it should be heavy enough that it will counter-balance the rod and line when in your hand but most fishermen prefer the outfit to be a little tip heavy, insisting they can feel it work better. A tiny ultra-light reel doesn't work well except on matching rods.

Fly reels can be had with handles on either the right or left side and for a right-handed caster there is merit in either setup. For many years I cranked on the left side but then switched over to the right when I learned I could crank about twice as fast with my right hand, a big help when fish came at me quickly and I had to hurry to keep the line taut. And I like to change the rod over now and then for a rest of the casting hand. But it's quicker to grab a reel handle on the left side and maybe you're more nearly ambidextrous than I am. It is a help to have a reel with an exposed spool rim so you can use your fingers to increase drag.

Reels with interchangeable spools are a help in switching lines and I preach the efficiency of specialized tapers and weights. If you're going to be a long way from the tackle store it's nice to have two reels in case you step on one. If they're exactly alike, so much the better.

Bass seldom run very far, and despite blood-curdling tales of bass battles, I have never had one get me down to the backing. Generally it's a matter of stopping him before he gets into something. However, the bass is capable of running and a truthful friend had one decide to stay on top for fifty or sixty yards. Big fish. In a lifetime of catching big bass on grass flats he swears it's the only long runner he's met. Anyway, a reel with considerable backing takes up line faster and a bass fisherman just might connect with something that sprints instead of yanks.

If the water's deep it's sometimes easy to run out of hands.

I think the best way to collect bass and panfish flies, bugs and streamers is to buy them as you need them. We'll discuss specific needs as we come to them but I don't think you need a four-inch Florida popping bug for smallmouths in a northern creek. Let's use some restraint on this. Most anglers carry unused flies and bugs around for years and such things simply accumulate. I do think you should pay some special attention to what I call compromise bugs and streamers. A #6 bug, for example, is a little small for bass and a little big for bluegills, but will catch them both. They make good probers on strange waters and when things are slow near home.

Since warm-water fishermen carry fewer things than the trout addict, many bass anglers do not have fishing vests at all, but a vest will keep most of your needs in one place and I like it.

Waders and boots can be selected to fit specific waters and we'll bring them in where needed. The same goes for boats and tube floats.

How to Use It

I see no reason why a beginner cannot cast well enough to go fly fishing within half an hour. A thirty-minute caster will not be ready to enter a casting tournament and he will probably tire if he tries to cast all day, but he should operate well enough to catch fish.

Bass and panfish do not require the delicacy often needed for educated trout and do not require the distance sometimes needed for salt-water fishing. If there's a difficult part it's in throwing bugs and streamers (especially bugs) that are highly wind-resistant. I have known trout fishermen who become disgusted with bass bugs within a few minutes but the difference in timing is easily solved. Technical analysis of the casting moves is unnecessary to begin with and can come later for those who seek perfection. Without starting from scratch, we can discuss some of the things that apply to bass in particular and if we touch basic casting no harm is done.

With the big flies used for bass a smooth pickup is essential, starting slow and gaining speed gradually. It's less critical with small flies. A jerky pickup is fatal with bass bugs; the rod must always be loaded smoothly. Floating lines must ride high on the water.

Most of the early dropouts in fly fishing quit after they have learned to throw an acceptable line, but find it is hard work. They still haven't quite mastered the timing, so casting for them is really pretty strenuous work. The time comes, though, when an average caster will find that his feet, legs, or sitting anatomy become tired before his arm or hand, even with heavy rods.

Few fly casters develop without some sort of instruction but few retain a resident teacher, and nothing helps as much as study

15

of the loop you're working with. They say "what goes up is what comes down" and we could modify that a little to "what goes back is what goes forward." I see many sloppy casters who never look back to see what their backcasts are doing. They're surprised when a backcast hits the water, ground, or the fellow paddling the canoe. There are all sorts of photos and drawings showing what a backcast should look like and you don't need a teacher to see what's going on back there.

You need a fairly small loop but casting style, rod, line weight, and fly size change things. Anyway, it should be a fairly smooth loop with a minimum of waves and no sharp bends. Most good loops ride fairly high.

It's best to learn casting with the rod's arc going straight over the casting shoulder but once that style has been achieved a large number of veterans tend to sideswipe a little—that is, the rod tips a little to the right for a right-handed caster. In theory at least, this is detrimental to accuracy, but apparently it is a restful motion. Some of those who use it at other times wave the rod straight forward and back when trying for pinpoint accuracy. They'd probably cast better if they always did it like that except when casting under something or fighting wind.

For a few hundred years there have been strict rules as to casting with the wrist only, the forearm only, or the entire arm. As a youth I was told that a real fly caster does it only with his wrist (that won't work for extreme distance) and much later I was shown a leather wrist gadget supposed to make it impossible to use the wrist without the forearm. Since true distance casters use wrist, forearm, and biceps and delicate anglers often use the wrist only, let's stay away from rules. Throw the loop right and the thing will go, even if you do it with your feet. I never said the wrist-locker wasn't helpful but a little variety is restful and as long as the loop curls out there where you want it you will be struck by no avenging lightning bolts. Extreme distance requires some special moves although I have known fine fishermen who caught fish through long lifetimes without knowing how to double-haul.

You must be able to shoot some line, of course. The usual procedure is to retrieve part of your casting distance, then pick up

With little room for a backcast, angler throws a bigger loop than usual.

the line and make a backcast, after which the rod is driven forward and some line released. That's "shooting" line. If you pull hard with your line hand (left hand for right-handers) as you make your fishing cast you increase distance. That's a single haul and is all most fishermen ever use.

The "double haul" was long considered a device of the master caster and it is a little tricky at first, being a little like patting your head and rubbing your stomach at the same time. It's not magic but should be left until the other moves are second nature. Even though a bass angler may not need it for extreme distance, it is a help in driving a big fly into a strong wind. You pick up your line from the water in the usual way and then feed line through the guides on your backcast. Now you have a somewhat longer loop back there than you'd ordinarily use. Then you pull line back through the guides *as the rod goes forward,* and release it. This adds to casting power and will help you shoot for distance. The double haul can be pretty long if you're reaching for the other side of the lake and a tournament distance caster swings his line hand clear down around his knee before releasing it. The double haul can be a lot of help—but you can also live without it.

If your outfit matches, you shouldn't need to do much false casting. A bass fisherman can work a shoreline from a boat or wade grass flats for hours with hardly any false casting, using a floating line. Remember that each false cast doubles your effort.

"Floating line" is a tricky term and the higher it sits on the water the easier it is to pick up and cast. Don't spare the fly-line "cleaner." Actually, it's generally a waterproofing material. With use, the line tends to pick up dirt that makes it lie low in the water and the pickup kills your cast, possibly even pulling a surface bug under. When your bug plops as you pick it up, either the line is tending to sink or your bug is riding the water wrong through poor design or damage from rough use. With shallow underwater streamers the pickup is a little less complex although the high-floating line is a help.

A friend of mine, who was a fine caster for years and strongly right-handed, had his right shoulder damaged in Vietnam and began left-handed casting. The rod work, he said, went fine, but he

When used for maximum distance, the double haul requires a very long pull with the line hand.

had a great deal of trouble teaching his right hand to do what his left hand had been doing all that time. I'm strongly right-handed too, but use my left hand in some casting emergencies; when I tried to learn full-time line handling with my right hand it remained sloppy.

Remember we're dealing much of the time with flies generally considered hard to cast. One of the finest trout and steelhead anglers I know went so far as to say *"nobody* can cast them well." Much of it is a matter of line handling.

Except in fairly swift rivers, the bass lure is nearly always kept moving with the line hand. After the cast is completed it should become second nature to take the line across a finger of the rod hand as it grips the rod handle. If you're a right-hander you now have the line securely in your left hand and looped over a finger of the right hand—fairly taut and ready to begin manipulation.

I always pull the line across the middle finger of my rod hand, simply because it's longer and grabs the line easier. Some use the forefinger and some pull the line across both. This decision does not change the world but you're going to do a lot of dragging that line across your finger in bass fishing, so be sure you do it the most comfortable way—for you. If you're stripping in line very fast you can hang on with your rod finger, then reach around it with the line hand, catch the taut line at the stripping guide, and haul in a lot of it—four feet at a pull—catching the line again with the "rod finger" and hauling again with the other hand.

With the line on the water, most of the manipulation of the fly is done in combination moves with both rod tip and the line hand. As he prepares to "work" his fly, the angler should point his rod tip just a little above it and the rod should be nearly parallel to the water. The common error is to work the fly too much with the rod and end up with the tip high in the air. In that position it is very difficult to set a hook as the tip has no place to go except back over the shoulder. I find it most convenient to have the rod tip pointed slightly to the right of the fly and slighty upward.

It's true that most of the fly manipulation is done with the line hand, but a fisherman quickly learns that a little twitch of the rod tip can do wonders, and he soon learns to take up the resultant

Most bass bug and fly operations are handled with line running through a finger of the rod hand and retrieved with the line hand.

With considerable loose line to handle, many fishermen hold it in their lips.

slack instantly. The only danger in using the rod tip for manipulation is that you can keep getting it too high and have nowhere to go when you set a hook, especially if the fish comes toward you.

In setting the hook, the rod tip is lifted—or pulled sidewise—at the same moment the line hand tightens up. I say "tightens up" because a hefty yank on the line, together with the rod lift, can put a lot of strain on things. The chances are you will be using a leader that tests six pounds or more—but a sudden yank will separate surprisingly heavy tackle. It is almost impossible to lift more than two or three pounds with a rod tip at right angles, but you can actually jerk several times that. Hook-setting is a quick lift, not a yank.

When fishing a bass bug with short pulls and twitches, it is difficult to avoid slack line as a strike comes. It's true comedy when a fisherman gets an explosive blast on a bug, finds his rod clear back "over his shoulder," and has several feet of slack between him and his target. The result is a tremendous yank that gets to the fish after it has discarded the bug and is looking for quarry somewhere else. Some fishermen keep doing this and simply don't see how it happens. Just keep the rod tip down until you get a strike and always take up the slack immediately after twitching or pulling a bug.

One of the first rules in playing a big, hard-running fish is to "get him on the reel," meaning that you can use the reel's drag so there's no danger of tangling loose line in the water, on the deck, or on the bank. This isn't easy if the fish won't run away from the rod. Many an angler has desperately tried to reel in his slack line while a bass explored the depths of a weed bed or came straight at him. One of my most humiliating moments came when I hooked a good bass while wading, tried to get him "on the reel," couldn't retrieve line fast enough as he came toward me and found he had wrapped me in my own line while other fishermen in a nearby boat collapsed in ribald laughter. Generally, a bass won't run so far that you must have him on the reel instantly. Use your line hand. When he's on the reel, exposed spool rims allow use of the hand to supplement a light drag.

With some long-running fish it is necessary to point the rod

Reel with exposed rim
enables fisherman to
supplement drag by using
fingers on spool.

nearly straight at them when they make hard rushes and you aren't
quite sure about the reel drag. I have never found this necessary
with bass. It helps to keep the rod well bent, and usually high. If
you try to keep a bass from jumping and the water is fairly open,
you can put the tip down and to one side. Let's not get into the
arguments for letting or not letting a bass jump. Some consider it a
matter of sportsmanship, and I like to see them jump, but if it's a
big one and the water is open, I may try to pull him over or stymie
the jump entirely.

Bass often throw flies, and especially bugs, but not as easily as
they toss heavy lures. You need a tight line while he's in the air to
prevent lure shaking, as the bass is good at that, but trying to "pull
him over" to stop the vibration must be done with restraint lest

24

you jerk the hook free. There are two kinds of bass jumps, the one in which the fish simply "swims into the air," generally going a little way nearly parallel to the water, and the real head-shaker that discards so many lures. The shaking jump usually starts very slowly, as the fish comes almost straight up, and there is a long instant in which the fish's head and gaping mouth are above the surface and almost motionless while the horsepower is being gathered for the leap. I once had a good fish close to me, needed it badly for a picture, and performed a sleight-of-hand trick that should have made me famous.

I had my rod tip high and well bent and had stuck one hand with the rod handle well behind me—only nine feet of leader and line out to the fish. Just as I started to hoist his head to the surface where I could grab his jaw, he came up and prepared to jump and shake his head—mouth wide open. At that instant the bug came out of his mouth, but since I had been ready to grab him anyway, I reached over and nabbed him by the lower lip. I had a witness too, and took a pretty picture of the fish. I report this, not only as an example of fool luck, but to show how long a bass primes himself before going straight up. The lip hold immobilizes bass pretty thoroughly.

Of course a boat fisherman can simplify things with a good-sized landing net but the wader will do almost as well catching his fish by the lip. He may need pliers occasionally. Bass are pretty tough customers and being too gentle in removing a hook might do more damage than good in the long run. A minor tear around the mouth is better than keeping him out of the water and probing at him. If you're releasing fish, I believe you'll find the smaller ones will take more abuse than the big ones. Stress can kill.

You need a heavy line to straighten out a loop and big fly for short distances and that's where the "bass taper" comes in. If you overload the rod a weight or two you can cast without getting quite all of the heavy part out, and for the short casts a big level line will work.

Very light rods are fine for casting small bugs and near-surface streamers but you need a #8 to scratch the bottom with a sinking

A lip hold generally works on bass but if it's a big one the fisherman is likely to be a little over-enthusiastic.

line and possibly a weighted fly. A huge, soggy nightmare of a bottom-bumper and fifty feet of sinking line come up better with a powerful rod.

It's good to dry out flies and bugs when you're through using them, especially those with very light hooks that can simply rust away—and there are places for light hooks. The reels are generally simple and easily serviced but should be stored dry. All rods should be dry when stored as corrosion can damage fittings. Most of us leave the heaviest section of leader attached to the line and simply change the forward part when it gets worn or knotted. Knots do wear and a large share of breakoffs come at over-aged splices in leaders.

Modern fly lines can take a lot of abuse but it is good to take them off the reel and store them in bigger loops when they aren't to be used for some time. I keep telling myself that but I seldom do it. The backing should be taken off the reel and straightened out from time to time; it's often stored wet and you never know when it's "cut in" on the spool and will be hard to get off in an emergency.

Wading fishermen will be happiest with vests. In or on a vest are extra leader material, pliers, a pair of scissors or nippers, a box for wet flies and a box for surface stuff, cleaner for the line, and some floatant for hair bugs or bug wings. Good place to keep sunglasses, insect dope, and even a miniature first-aid kit. A raincoat and jacket go in the back pocket and you can go on from there, fishing vests being known as treasure troves of useless and often unrecognizable gadgets, and sometimes long-forgotten sandwiches.

Storage is simple.

Bugs, Flies, and Lures

3

Early American fly fishermen went to the upstart bass from trout and salmon so the first flies used for the latter were generally simply oversized wet trout flies and streamers. Bass got their very own attractors somewhere around 1910 when Peckinpaugh enlarged some cork-buoyed flies he had been using for bluegills.

Those first bugs had double hooks but single-hooked bugs were most popular within only a few years. Bug bodies are made of wood (generally balsa), cork, plastic, and hair, and the general types break down simply.

The true "popper" has either a cupped head or one that is flat in front. The "slider" has a bullet-shaped head. The "skipper" front slopes forward and up from the water. Most fishermen can get enough noise from a bug without the cup. Hair bugs began as simple "powder puffs" of deer hair but in recent years have been built to pop, dive, or dart.

Some anglers used to small flies have trouble getting the timing right with bugs, but if the rod has enough power that should be straightened out in a few minutes. In choosing bugs it's important to check their planing qualities. "Planing" simply means the way the thing rides in the air during casting. Most bass bugs are big, generally #4 or larger, but in trying for greater size we need to rely on extra length rather than breadth, which builds wind resistance. You can cast a four-inch bug (tail and all) with a #8 rod very easily, but if you insist on an inch-wide head the wind resistance will beat your cast down. For a time there were some imaginative bugs whomped up by artistic makers, looking beautiful in the box but too broad and too heavy for practical use. They ranged from

mouthy frogs to fat mice. Recent models are generally more practical.

Bug weight must be kept down and the deer-hair models are
lightest of all. A #4 deer-hair bug can be made to work with a #6
rod and I've used that combination on a great many smallmouths.
Imitation frogs in the proper color work with hair, feather, or plastic legs, but be careful about the frog's mouth. You don't need a
big one to make it pop. New bugs should be checked for hook bite
and you should be able to hang them in a screenwire. If the hook is
too protected by the body, it can usually be bent to a wider gap.
Hooks of light wire may not last long but they sure cast better and
light-wire hooks are much easier to set.

Bugs with hard bodies (wood, cork, or plastic) are most likely
to hook and dive deep when picked off the water. If one does this
consistently, ruining a cast and sounding like a drowning horse, it's
out of balance, the front or "cup" has the wrong shape, or a
heavy, sinking leader and poorly floating line pull it under. Bugs
must be picked up with a gradually accelerating lift of the rod because, after all, this is about as bulky a thing as you're likely to
cast.

The hair bug has changed rapidly in recent years, and many of
them have been designed to dive slightly, a "lip" being formed
from stiff hair and usually varnished or glued to keep it that way.
Probably the best-known design is the Dahlberg Diver but there
are many other "lipped" ones. Here you have something that per-
forms like many spinning and baitcasting plugs, can have considerable bulk, yet retains lightness for fly casting.

Sometimes a poorly tied hair bug does better than a master's
product, simply because ragged ends create attractive effects in the
water. I have found the ragged bug often superior with largemouth
bass but it has had less advantage in my experience with smallmouths, which may be pure coincidence. A commercial fly tyer of
many years ago tied ragged bugs for his friends and neat ones for
the market. The deadly ragged ones wouldn't sell. Some of the
most beautiful hair bugs are tightly tied and can be trimmed to
almost any shape.

For bass and most panfish the addition of rubber legs, strands

At left is a hair bug with cupped head, an early form of diver. Third from left is a "skipper."

The Dahlberg Diver, shown here in a weedless model, is designed to perform much like diving plugs; its head can be shaped to give a variety of actions.

of hair, or waving feathers improves catches. I have tested this pretty carefully, in one case we took some beautifully done hair bugs, tightly tied and perfectly trimmed, and tried them against the same thing with the addition of rubber legs, the latter winning in number of strikes by a wide margin. This was on largemouth bass and the bugs were fished slowly, giving the "extensions" time to wave seductively. For me, the faster the bug is worked the less help the legs can be and when yanking big bugs loudly for salt-water fish I could find no help at all in legs. Most of them cause little casting trouble since they are flexible enough to become streamlined in the air.

Bug color isn't considered important by many veterans since most of the tasteful designs are on top where the fish can't see them. Sure, sure, the bass can't admire the frog back or topside minnow fins but he can certainly get an overall picture that varies with color, especially light and dark. A Michigan lake test with white deer-hair bugs against natural ones showed the white ones as big winners on smallmouths. On largemouths farther south I couldn't see much difference but some friends insisted the natural gray-brown color worked better. Some largemouth fishermen still farther south used a bumblebee-colored hard-bug body for years— and then switched to a frog color almost altogether. Don't get carried away, but colors can make a difference tomorrow.

Gleam and glitter can help with bugs as well as with other lures. For generations, sequins have been stuck to hard-bug bodies and more recently we have been using Mylar products under various trade names. These glitter strands are great as long as they are very fine, but coarse strands of glitter material will make work out of casting and sound like a strafing attack in the air. There have been some fanciful bugs, including those with holes all the way through for water to burble in and some that wound up rubber bands during casting and then did their own swimming. I think all of them caught fish—sometimes.

In between bugs and streamers are some highly productive things, and probably we should classify the "divers" here. Careful use of floatant solutions can make something like the Muddler Minnow into a high-floating bug or a surface-film navigator that

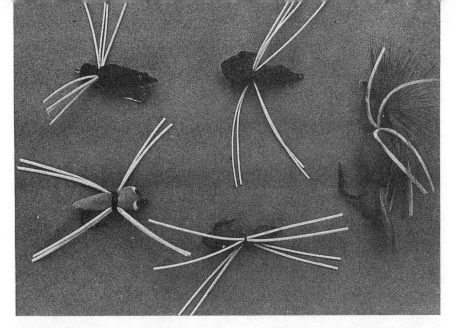

Sponge-rubber bugs with rubber legs are fragile but among the most productive of panfish lures.

Bass bug and fly designs. A modified Muddler Minnow is second from top at right. At bottom center is the Marm, a minnow imitation useful for schooling bass. At center is the hard-to-cast but effective Dragon Fly.

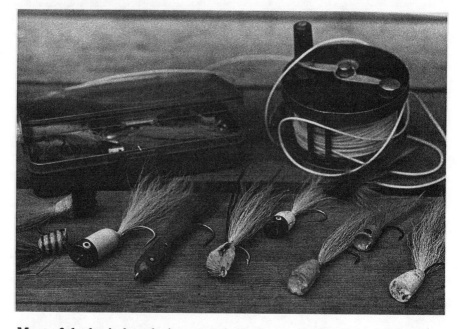

Most of the basic bug designs are shown here, ranging from "diving" heads to sliders, skippers, and deep cups.

darts like a minnow or jerks about like a grasshopper. I have used a bit of cork halfway back on a big streamer to make it a sloshy surface creature and found my associates laughed at it and the fish it caught. I called it the Slosher and it works well with a weedguard in thick stuff. It is not as well known as the Royal Coachman or the Muddler Minnow but I still have it around here somewhere. Some artificial frogs have been made with sloping noses that caused them to dive a little if pulled fast and a bit of pork rind fastened to a hard body produces a nameless killer on some special occasions.

True streamers are imitations of small fish and I know of no patterns that will not take bass on occasion. Generally, we try to give an appearance of length and the use of some full-length dark material adds to the fishy look. The "Blonde" series involves a double tie—usually made of bucktail. One bunch of hair is tied in

34

at the head end and a second is fastened back near the bend of the hook, making a much longer fly than is possible with a single bunch of hair. As with most bass flies there are almost as many variations as there are tyers. Most streamers have slim tinsel bodies.

Few of our favorite streamers are chosen through true tests and I'm afraid we pick the ones that look prettiest to us. My own first choice is what I call a Silver Outcast. It's a rather simplified form of the Silver Doctor with some strands of peacock herl that run full length and suggest a baitfish's lateral line. A few glitter strands help too, and if I had only one streamer the Outcast would be it. But any Silver Doctor streamer with added herl and glitter

Tried and true bass streamers. At top is the Silver Outcast and at far left is one of the Blonde series. Bead head on white streamer gives jigging action. Lower streamer shows fine Mylar strands.

would be just as good. Many good streamers are tied with sides of silver-pheasant feathers and with jungle cock "cheeks." The Gray Ghost and Black Ghost are two of the best known of smallmouth streamers in both rivers and lakes. A streamer is not an exact imitation and exact patterns are less important than general impression, depth, and overall length. They can be weighted easily with strip or wire lead and near the front this gives jiglike action.

The Phillips bead-headed streamers have a slight jig action when retrieved by stripping and the longer the pauses between strips the deeper the dive. Jig action is most important when a streamer is running fairly deep, either through its own weight or with a sinking line or sinking tip. A good streamer man I have fished with kept a roll of strip lead at hand constantly and continually added or subtracted from the weight at his streamer's head. The exact opposite, of course, is the "floating streamer," which leaves a wake through various kinds of cover.

Somewhere in the classification of flies are the wormlike feather or plastic things that come close to the true plastic worm of the baitcasting and spinning rods. Most of these are fished at considerable depth but I've used them on top at night. The synthetic hair (FisHair is a trade name) can be made into a long and slender "eel" that's easy to cast and wriggles when retrieved or while sinking. I have had mediocre success with fly-rod worms and mine haven't looked as good to the fish as they did to me. Of course you can use the real plastic number and flop it around with the fly rod but this isn't really fly casting—and it's too heavy and fragile to ride through much air travel. Bug tails, streamers, and "worms" made of some leathers deteriorate rapidly and one bug and fly maker states that "leather isn't compatible with water." Depends on how it was treated in tanning. Rabbit skin hasn't lasted well for me.

Streamer size depends partly upon fish size but three-inchers are about average. You can go much longer for largemouths and I've used little one-inchers for schooling bass working on small bait. I avoid giving exact hook sizes since hooks come in so many shapes and lengths and vary with manufacturers. A 4/0 is about as large as you'll ever want; hook weight has considerable bearing on streamer depths. Some good fishermen for really big largemouths use hooks as small as #6. Heavy hooks will demand streamer bulk for planing purposes. "Planing" in the air is one of the most underrated factors in fly construction. Casting a heavy bare hook will convert almost anyone to study of planing problems. Call it "air buoyancy" if that sounds better.

Fish strike streamers from all angles. A bass is supposed to attack the front end of fast-moving prey but I think the hook should be a third as long as the streamer and some fishermen, plagued by tail nibbles, use two hooks in tandem. It's seldom considered but a leader can ward off front-end strikes to some extent from some angles, the leader pushing the hook away; extra hook length may help here. There are days when you seem to hook them all and days when you miss most of them. They may take differently tomorrow. Setting the hook with fast-stripped streamers

If a bug will not hang on a screenwire, the hook lacks enough "bite" for satisfactory striking.

is a pretty simple tug but you can miss fish when allowing streamers to sink on too much slack. Keep the line almost taut and the hooks sharp.

When we get into nymphs or streamers that really skim the bottom there's a limit as to just how far down we want to go. Many of us have fished much deeper but after we get more than about eight feet down the rigs become more awkward to handle and only the dedicated prefer the fly rod. Spinning and plugging gear are generally more efficient down there.

Some of the best deep-going things are truly impressionistic—that is, they aren't very good copies of any particular living creature but have some of the general characteristics. They tend to be soft, squirmy, and dark-colored. There are flies definitely imitating the cottus or sculpin, a rather low order of fish that's noted as trout and smallmouth prey, but these flies work in many places where there are no sculpins. A good example of the sculpin imitator is the dark-colored Muddler Minnow, often customized until it has little resemblance to the original.

The Woolly Worms have caught a wide variety of panfish for me, in addition to bass, and the Bitch Creek and Woolly Booger are really only sport-model Woolly Worms. In most cases the sizes smaller than #6 have not taken the larger bass. On chilly Florida days when nothing else worked I used dressed-up Woolly Worms for a grab bag of panfish and small bass from the bottom along shallow, weedy banks. There were some good-sized shellcrackers (red-ear sunfish), which aren't noted for taking artificials. My retrieves were a series of twitches with a sinking-tip line.

Exact imitation in these bottom searchers seems to be handicap rather than a help, the same as with surface lures. The most learned of fish biologists can't explain this but meticulous artificial nymphs, molded from the real thing, have not done as well as rather vague imitations, and such experiments have been going on as long as there have been fly rods. A good example concerns the hellgrammite, a formidable-appearing larval stage of the dobson fly. Many fishermen don't realize it isn't a fully developed creature and it has been a mainstay bait for smallmouth fishermen. Harry Murray relates how a nearly exact replica doesn't do as well as an impressionistic nymph, but he explains how the real thing does some athletic maneuvers the near-duplication can't, and how a more flexible imitation at least pretends to be alive.

Deep nymphs and streamers are generally fished at least partly dead drift in strong current, employing some line-mending and minor movement. Anything resembling a nymph works best for bass when moved very slowly in still or nearly still water. The ways of getting it down and keeping it down need attention. Many casters who think they are really working the bottom are simply sinking their fly to it and bringing it quickly to the surface on the retrieve. This happens regularly when a floating line is used and even a sinking-tip line won't keep something near the bottom if retrieved rapidly.

Nine-tenths of shoreline fishing involves casting toward the bank from farther out, and keeping a deep-going fly on the bottom or very near it requires either a delicate touch or black magic. Casting from the bank and retrieving the fly up the slope toward it makes it possible to retain a predetermined depth. With deep flies the ideal location is usually just above the bottom and that's easiest with a buoyant fly and a sinker a few inches up the leader from it, the leader actually dragging the bottom on the retrieve. This is an unhappy combination to cast although some have made a science of it with short throws.

We all love to relate instances in which thoughtful fly selection and application have resulted in big catches but sordid failure deserves some consideration too. For fifteen years I have been using a sinking shooting head and casting shiny little flies for shad in a Florida river. I know that the things are right at the bottom and that they catch shad all right. I do the casting from a sod bank and there is a firm bottom several feet down. It's a good bass area and I have caught plenty of bass along the sod banks where there is a little weedy fringe, using bugs in most cases. You'd think largemouth bass would beat the shad to the bottom-bumpers, but in fifteen years I have caught fewer than a dozen bass—and those were small. They ignore those deep flies but take bugs along the banks where the deep flies are picked up on each cast. It shakes my faith.

Maine smallmouth that came up from deep granite boulders to take a small streamer.

Strike indicators are important when long leaders and floating lines are used for fairly deep flies. Starting with a high-floating and highly visible line, you can use a piece of bright fluorescent leader butt section and then use little commercial tabs attached farther along toward the fly. Some use as many as three. Others use bright-colored yarn tied into the knots of tapered leaders. Indicators pay off.

Until the advent of spinning there were many fly fishermen who used miniature plugs, spoons, and spinners. Generally, these things work better with spinning but a tiny willowleaf spinner isn't hard to cast with a powerful rod and can spice up a streamer. As a youth I caught a great many bass and panfish with a Pflueger Luminous Tandem Spinner, a terrible thing to cast on a fly rod but not much worse than some of the combinations used today for bottom bumping. Frankly, spinners are taboo among many fly casters who insist it "isn't fly fishing." They may be right but some of them throw sinkers and leadcore lines that are even harder to cast.

The term "strip-casting" is almost forgotten today and involves coiling considerable loose line and throwing something heavy that pulls it through the guides as in baitcasting or spinning. I've seen it used on everything from half-ounce spoons to shiners but that certainly isn't fly casting. It's an emergency measure.

Bass streamers and bugs are easy to make and a good-sized streamer is the first product of many budding fly tyers. For many, catching fish on their own creations is much of the fun. Since nearly all bass flies and bugs may be called "impression" lures, there are thousands of variations from named patterns. Many big fly boxes are crowded with unnamed things and their makers sometimes build no two alike. Nearly all of the materials are available at low cost from dealers since exotic furs and feathers are not necessary.

Bugs are easy to make and there are instruction books and magazine articles that will steer the novice. However, when dealing with cork or wood-bodied bugs, home construction is seldom an economy measure. Unless you turn out quite a number of them, the individual bug takes more time than it's worth. Economy of time and money can be bypassed, however, when a fisherman has

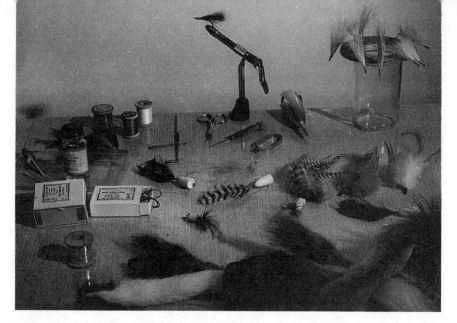

Materials for making bass bugs and streamers are simple and not expensive.

something really special in mind. In my case, for example, we found extremely light hooks helpful in some bugs, but they wouldn't have been durable enough for commercial manufacture. We have modified many bugs by adding rubber legs and have deliberately hacked up beautiful hair creations to make them more attractive. Some of the best ones look second-hand to begin with. We have installed monofilament and wire weed-guards on many commercial bugs. We've added and subtracted feather and hair from streamers and nymphs. Remember that bass lack artistic tastes.

Where and When

There are so many kinds of bass water and bass methods that two bass fishermen meeting for the first time often have little in common. Admittedly, there are bass waters where the fly rod is tough to use and less productive than other methods. There also are waters where the fly rod has never been given a fair trial and you can't always tell by looking.

Proper water temperature, of course, is one of the requirements of bass livelihood. Smallmouth bass generally occupy cooler water, but there are many lakes and streams where they are found along with largemouth bass. Bass become accustomed to a wide variety of temperatures and can be active in a northern lake with a chill that would probably cause them to become near-dormant in the South. I do not know what would be the coldest temperature at which either the smallmouth or the largemouth would strike a fly, but I have some disconcerting examples. I'll mention one that took place in central Florida on a slow-moving river.

We fished on the Florida river during a chilly snap but didn't realize how cold it had gotten. We'd had a personal rule not to bother with fish in those waters when the water temperature got below 55 degrees and some of our friends insisted that it be 65 (not cold at all for some northern states). Fishing was terrible. After two hours without a strike I finally got out the thermometer. The water temperature was 46 degrees and we laughed ruefully as we prepared to head for the boat ramp, but before I could crank up, my partner had a solid bass strike on a near-surface streamer. We saw the fish plainly although it got away. Since then I have been very wary about flat statements concerning temperatures. Bass adapt.

Largemouth bass spawning takes place all the way from February to early summer, depending upon geography and the thermometer. If the temperature isn't right the female fish can absorb the eggs and abort the program. Some of the best fishing of the year is just prior to spawning and while it is actually in progress. The matter of actually fishing when bass are "on the beds" gets arguments. Largemouth bass like shallow, firm bottoms. Smallmouths spawn much deeper most of the time. The male fish makes a "nest" and after the female deposits the eggs and they are fertilized the male guards them. Really large fish are invariably females. I don't know how big a largemouth male can get but in the South a five-pounder would be a monster.

In most bass waters there is a great deal of temperature difference between early morning and midday, and when the weather is chilly for a given area the early afternoon is a good time. Early morning and late evenings are generally best and when it's really hot there's seldom much doing on artificials except near dawn and dusk. I believe more fly-rod bass are caught in late evening than at any other time, partly because there are more fishermen then and partly because the fish begin to move after the sun sinks. I have found early morning even better in hot weather, but if it's cool I'll take evening.

For some reason I have caught a great many fish around five o'clock in the afternoon in several parts of the country. I have no explanation for this, since the sun may still be high and the evening activity hasn't started. If I sound vague on these matters it's on purpose—for I lack the conviction of some anglers who will tell you exactly when to fish.

Do I believe in the solunar tables? Yes, except that there are a whole list of weather factors that can overpower them. I say the scheduled "feeding periods" are the time to fish, "other things being equal." I am sold on sudden barometric changes producing good fishing and have noted poor fishing when a high barometer is too persistent. These things are general, but let's get specific about flies, most of which are worked near or on the surface. Deep-fished flies can be necessary when water is too cold or too warm.

Many fine fishermen talk of "fly-fishing season" regarding bass

and panfish and they're thinking of the times when fish are especially active and willing to come to surface or near-surface lures.
However, if you want to gouge the bottom for either largemouth
or smallmouth bass you can use your fly rod at almost any time
bass feed. I recommend fly fishing near the bottom when necessary, but here we must face a fact avoided by the true fly-rod
faithful—there are times and places when other methods are much
better. Most of us don't live a constant fishing contest and you'll be
happier if you concede the superiority of other methods at times.

In testing a bottom-bumping fly-rod method, two of us once
used a baitcasting rod and a plastic worm as monitor. Those
largemouths liked the plastic worm better but they'd take the fly
when it was handled just right. Our idea was that we wouldn't
waste time with the fly where they wouldn't take the worm. The fly
caught a lot of fine bass but the worm caught more. Did the fly
fail? I don't think so, but not everyone would be willing to do
things the hard way. There are times when the fly rod will outdo
other methods and to use it only when it works well is no disgrace,
even though some of us diehards stick with it through thick and
thin. Call it a challenge if you want to—even though some observ-
ers will say you're "trying to train fish."

Oh, there *is* such a thing as "fly-fishing season" for bass, varying with the location. In the North, it comes in early summer, even
though flies will work until cold weather. In early June I've seen
Maine smallmouths come a long way up for a hair bug and if
weather is warm that's a very good time. In the Midwest ponds,
my best largemouth fishing with bugs has been well into the summer and very late in the evenings. In California lakes, early summer has been very good and fall has produced well too. If I had to
choose a time for Florida lake fishing I'd like it in early spring,
morning and evening.

Bass are most aggressive around spawning time and they feed
up before going on the beds. They'll strike well when spawning is
under way. Where big females can be seen on nests they can sometimes be annoyed into grabbing almost anything and some very
large catches are made that way—a system that's *too* successful at
times.

45

Night fishing can be good with some bugs that might be too noisy in daytime. Keep the casts short and there's no reason why darkness must be a problem with a fly rod. Some good night results are had on resort lakes where there's too much boat traffic in daytime, the fish adapting their program to speedboats and water skis. Large streamers serve at night but most fly fishermen work the surface. When bass school on top, flies are good at any time of year.

Types of bass water overlap but it can be classified to some extent. Largemouths tend to live in vegetation throughout their range, and although smallmouths like it too they're also addicted to rocky shorelines where vegetation is sparse. Where they live together in rivers, the smallmouths choose more current. Long ago, when fishing the Ozark mountain streams of Arkansas and Missouri, we'd find some of the best largemouth fishing in sloughs off the river proper while the smallmouths rose above and below the swift "shoals" and in the slower-moving pools with "chunk rock." Most of those rivers have been stilled by dams now and the best fly fishing on impoundments tends to be in the shallow coves. They don't build so many power dams these days but when the big lakes were new the fly fishing was good in sunken treetops. Some of the old trees last a long time.

Farm ponds can be managed for largemouth bass as well as for panfish, and although the balance can be precarious, some of the world's best fly fishing for bass is found in "tanks" that a long cast will almost reach across. Thousands of hurrying anglers drive past thousands of miles of roadside ditches that contain largemouth bass of all sizes. Fishing roadside ditches can be hard, weed-smashing work but a bass can get just as big there as he can in Lake Michigan or Lake Okeechobee. It takes prospecting, but the ditches can pay off and the fly rod is ideal for that job, flipping lures over cattails or weeds.

Some of the least-known bass fishing is that in brackish water, partly because it is so inconsistent. North Carolina's Currituck Sound is an old bass fishery, generally ideal for the bass bug. When I first heard of it most of the fishing was around duck blinds. Then, hurricanes changed it into an enormous grass flat with guides using

Ozark smallmouth stream where dead-drifted nymphs and streamers are effective in slow runs.

double-ended paddles on flat-bottomed boats. But fishing has fallen off badly lately with some of the best grass beds gone—current results of the vagaries of nature.

Another kind of brackish-water bass fishing requires constant study. With several years of good rainfall there'll be good bass crops in shallow coastal rivers, and when dry weather comes the bass will be forced down into water too salty for propagation. I've seen this condition several times in Florida's Everglades when the fishing has become almost too good. If drought continues the bass will perish. If rains come, they'll go back up into areas hard to reach by boots or boats. With several seasons of heavy rains the ordinarily salt-water reaches may turn fresh and grow the right kinds of vegetation. I have seen both of these conditions in the upper rivers of Everglades National Park, but they can occur in many other places—unheralded and possibly not even fished. A

47

Fishing Currituck Sound, best-known of the brackish-water bass areas. Such areas tend to be feast or famine, tide and weather causing the ups and downs.

fly-rod fanatic can mix maps with weather reports and sometimes have super bass fishing all to himself.

It may be that the best bass fishing I've ever had was at the head of a river in Everglades National Park, when a local guide told me that conditions were just right. There'd been the required high water for a time in the Glades, then the required dry weather to force the bass down.

It was mangrove country, where we had snook, tarpon, red-fish, and weakfish, and it was a long boat run upriver. The water had been fresh for long enough that fresh-water weeds and grasses were beginning to clog the stream and when the outboard bogged down in grass and we stopped to clear it we began to hear popping strikes along the shorelines. On each side of the river there was a bit of open water next to the mangrove banks. Our guide said it would be better farther up. Some of the strikes were too big for bass.

"Tarpon and snook, and maybe redfish," the guide said, but we were after bass. Far upstream, the guide explained, the Glades water was getting low and the fish had no place to go back there unless there was rain. We finally stopped where the shoreline strikes were almost constant. My friend made a short cast against the mangrove roots with a yellow popping bug—white tail. He let it rest for a moment but before he could twitch it wakes converged on it from all sides. There was a sort of cooperative strike and he hooked a ten-inch bass. Bigger ones chased it to the boat. It was like that all day and now and then there would be a big salt-water fish.

The fishing was too good to be challenging but we tried different kinds of bugs and some weedless streamers and I suppose such an orgy is good for the soul occasionally. Why, someone wanted to know, did we bother with two-pound bass when there were fifty-pound tarpon and other tackle-tearers in with them? I have no answer except that I had been a bass fisherman for a long time and the malady is incurable.

Then the fishing slowed. For some reason the bass turned off as bass do almost everywhere, but my wife Debie and I hadn't had enough. We went back up that river the next day, a fifty-mile run, and we camped in a high-sided old aluminum sixteen-footer. There is no dry land there but we could hang some of our gear in trees to make sleeping room. All night long the boat rocked gently as bass struck along its sides, the pops amplified by the bonging aluminum.

And the next morning I waded wet in warm Everglades water and the bass sucked in my bugs, slashed them and banged them. And the story had a happy ending for it rained soon and those fish could go back into the sawgrass to raise families. We saw no other fishermen and I extend this story because it is an example of opportunistic fishing in and near brackish water. Many such opportunities are missed and those who enjoy them are likely to be close-mouthed on the subject. Seek and ye shall find—part of the time, at least. We have been back to the heads of those rivers many times, and seldom have conditions been just right—but sometimes we strike it.

Millions of bass have perished in water too salty for their survival. When there are floods inshore they tend to migrate to sea. I believe in most cases that they simply make short migrations that end disastrously when the fresh water is met by too much salt. Of course some brackish-water bass live where they could not spawn successfully and it is the same with panfish such as bluegills or warmouth perch. I do not believe that any of these fish have true saltwater strains that go to sea and back as the trouts, striped bass, and others do. I think the reports of bass at sea simply cover fish that have inadvertently been washed out there.

The black bass is an opportunist, ever seeking to extend its range, and it can be expected to make a mistake now and then.

Some Special Moves

5

W hat scares a bass into headlong flight today may look like an easy meal to him tomorrow. On a single cast with surface lures you can run through the complete repertoire of lure performance.

Let it lie for a while. Some say to leave it there until the little rings of wake disappear, but you can wait longer than that. Still-fishing a bug is pretty boring if there's no current. Leave it a while anyway.

When you think it has been lying there too long, move it gently—very gently. If it has hair or feathers there will be a little squirming. Rubber legs will wave a little.

Next, you retrieve it a little way with a minimum of fuss, trying to give it a swimming action. Keep it coming smoothly for a few feet and then stop it.

Leave it there for a few seconds and then twitch it gently, let it pause, and then twitch it a few more times.

In conclusion, yank it hard and if it pops make it throw some water, almost too logical for bug fishing.

Most of us have seen bass hooked in clear water. It's common for fish to come over and watch something that has just struck the surface, even if he doesn't take it. Then, the progressively more violent manipulation may bring a strike. In the end, if it scares him away nothing's lost because he wasn't going to strike anyway.

Few fishermen have the patience to leave a surface bug completely still for long, but most of us remember leaving one there for some time while untangling something or fetching a sandwich and having a fish take the bug as it floated without movement. Chances are the bass had been watching the thing ever since it struck the water. I didn't believe in still-fishing a bug until I was humiliated on a Kansas tank pond.

"Tank pond" in that country doesn't mean a livestock watering hole. Tank ponds were impounded from small creeks in order to furnish water for steam railroad locomotives and the ponds stayed when the steam went. I returned to that Kansas pond after a long absence and met another fisherman where I launched my cartop boat. He had a homemade craft made from the gasoline wing tanks of a World War II airplane and he set up a good fly rod. The wind was hard out of the south and I don't think that influenced the day's events but I can't forget it.

I started drifting and casting with a bug I twitched and popped. The man in the wing tank rowed out to the center of the pond (there was underwater growth across nearly all of it), threw his bug out downwind, leaned back on a cushion and poured himself a cup of coffee. His "Dragon Fly" was a yellow cork body with white wings fanned out on each side, the whole thing almost two inches across. Using one is similar to casting a bow tie. He left it bobbing on the waves with his fly rod across his knees. He began catching bass almost immediately and played them with the calm of long experience. He never twitched his bug.

I dug out a Dragon Fly but I didn't have enough anchor and my little boat kept moving. I lost one good fish while he harvested a stringer-full, waves providing action for his bug. It made a wake, of course, with no casting and no disturbance from the boat. This works better on small waves than in smooth current. The expert stayed in one spot and probably there was some sort of bottom or weed formation he knew of there. I don't even know if he was a good caster for he just flopped the bug out a few feet and then leaned back.

I believe the most technical fly fishing I have ever seen was for largemouth bass, a statement likely to bring forth the outraged ghosts of great trout fishermen. In most cases, the "technical" part was involved with fish very near to the bottom and unwilling to

A sneaky trick with a hair bug. After it has caused the lily pad to quiver, it can be twitched off into the water. It works—sometimes.

change their depth. One such performance was conducted by Forrest Ware, a fisheries biologist and a veteran coaxer of stubborn largemouths. It was on a small but fairly deep Florida impoundment and resulted from patient experimentation.

I tried to catch fish on that lake with streamers, bugs, and big nymphs, using a floating line, and suspected there were no bass there. Ware caught them by the dozen and demonstrated his rig for me.

The fly was an enormous black Muddler Minnow on a short leader and he used a carefully dressed line with a sinking tip. Between the fly line and his leader was a short section of leadcore. The water was several feet deep and he used the floating part of his line as a strike indicator. He retrieved the rig gently with his fingertips and a "strike" usually appeared as a little quiver or gentle twitch of the floating line. I watched him catch a dozen bass up to around seven pounds; then I brought out a sinking shooting head with a flourish. If the bass wanted a big fuzzy black thing on the bottom I'd give it to them. I caught nothing with a short leader and a duplicate of Forrest's fly. I changed leader length, retrieving speed, and my place in the boat. Nothing.

Another bottom, another depth, and another bunch of bass would want everything a little different. Unique combinations can get results when conditions are tough—sometimes. Although my shooting head was a flop, I might in time have come to what Ware had—or something else that would work—but I'd still have the dainty takes. Did I miss some on my shooting head?

Most good bass lures are the result of trial and error, thought and patience. When I find a lake or river that simply won't produce for me I think of the "blank" water where Ware could catch fifty pounds of bass a day.

Underwater operations tend to require the most thought and scheming, exact depth being much of the answer, along with fly choice and speed. I once watched a small school of good-sized bass on a deep, clear shoreline of California's Lake Shasta, seven fish that cruised back and forth along a point as if looking for something. They were eight or ten feet down and wouldn't change their level, but when I got the exact depth they took willingly and in a

A patch of reeds in fairly open water can attract bass as well as the bait they feed on. This largemouth took a noisy popper.

highlight of my career I caught five of them, hooking one each time they passed. I had beached a boat and was casting from shore.

Most lake fishing is done along shorelines, the easiest places to find depth variations. We sometimes get so sold on working as close to the edge as possible that we neglect water that's just a little deeper. And it takes only a few switches of his tail for a bass to change his depth a great deal, something he can do several times a day for temperature, light, or feeding reasons. Fly fishermen can take lessons from plug and spinning fishermen—who can regulate their fishing depth more easily—retrieving up the shoreline as they cast from the bank, or letting a lure sink gradually when they cast from offshore, it's harder with flies and nymphs.

In really thick surface stuff we may use weedless bugs or

55

Fishing "edges" doesn't necessarily mean the bank. Here fish are being caught at a dropoff just off a shoreline weedbed invisible from offshore.

streamers with guards made of wire, heavy monofilament, or stiff hair. Some very good bass bugs have been made with the hook's barb riding up, and some can skitter over lily pads and through eelgrass tips with hardly any hangups.

In heavy grass or weeds, everything is connected and a yank on a stubborn hangup can alert fish thirty feet away because the whole underwater landscape moves. A fish might leave but if the movements are just right he might be attracted. Waders and boaters should remember their activities are not only telegraphed through the water, as elsewhere, but can cause all of the cover to jostle or crawl.

In most cases, fishing in weeds should be done very slowly, for even if a fish wants to strike he may not actually find the lure immediately. Residents sometimes come for considerable distance, their progress noted by gentle weed or grass movements, often

Lily-pad water requires careful manipulation to avoid hangups—and hooked fish must be handled with firmness. This angler's hooking form is perfect.

57

Short casts and heavy leaders are necessary in weeds thicker than most anglers would bother with.

causing me to strike viciously—too soon.

Usually, there are open pockets where a surface lure can be worked; there's a premium on something that can make a little fuss without moving very far, avoiding hangups. Generally, bass will not break through a surface mat of weeds—but they look for little gaps of some kind. Strikes nearly always come in the openings, however small. When eelgrass and similar single-bladed grasses protrude from the surface the fish will part it to strike, but they still prefer the little gaps.

Where the fodder is especially thick, I've used a long, weedless streamer with a little cork float around the middle. It floats mushily and makes a wake. It isn't revolutionary.

For a few decades it never occurred to me that a weed fisherman learns special casts without thinking about it—and then I went fishing in some lily-pad water with a top caster who had never

A bass fisherman sometimes looks like an ambusher but there are some open places in the heavy cover.

Back country? Hardly. These canoeists are operating in a roadside ditch along a busy highway.

fished that kind of cover before. He seemed to have tough luck, being hung up frequently, while I seemed to get along all right. Then it dawned that I was taking some instinctive measures that were standard operating procedures among my bonnet-busting friends.

For lily pads you need a high-floating line and a short leader, preferably doped. Anything that sinks will lead your lure into the notch where the stem joins the pad part and chances are you'll have to float or wade over to unhook it. When your fly is in an open spot, a quick lift will probably get it airborne—but if it is among thick bonnets a gentle retrieve is likely to get it through. Bonnets are strong but will move aside with gentle pressure. A cross wind complicates things and long casts are asking for trouble. This is the place for your more powerful rods with heavy leaders; there isn't much finesse needed.

I knew a fellow who repeatedly won big-fish contests by using a large bug with a small one as a trailer about two feet back. The big one popped and the little one was a dull-colored nondescript on a #10 hook that caught a lot of panfish a well as some whopping bass. His theory is that the noisy bug attracted fish that might not care to eat it but accepted the miniature with enthusiasm.

There's another use for trailers or droppers when dealing with "schooling bass," largely a product of the South. School bass will operate on lakes where they chase bait schools and streams where the bottom or bank conformation confuses migrating schools of a variety of small species. If the baitfish are very small you can create your own school by casting several little streamers on the same leader, making short casts over the "schooling ground" and dancing your streamers across the surface.

Most fly fishermen have caught so many bass with rough-and-tumble methods that we simply don't bother to use finer terminal tackle on slow days. I don't say that smallmouths are necessarily harder fish to fool than largemouths but they often live in water that demands more care. Most of the more delicate smallmouth fishing is in streams where current plays a big part in presentation. You've probably caught bigmouths in boiling rapids—occasionally—but they generally prefer sluggish current or no current at all.

I believe more bass are scared by lines and leaders in the air than in the water. Anglers meeting large fish for the first time may be astonished to see a 150-pound tarpon apparently fleeing from a flying three-inch streamer. Since so large a fish probably can't even remember when there was a bird big enough to eat him, it seems ridiculous.

But what drove the tarpon to deep water probably wasn't a tiny fly descending on him but the leader or line or both, which gave off flashes of reflected light as they snaked toward him. Having imperfect vision of things seen through the surface, it is quite possible the tarpon thought he was watching sun glancing off a twenty-foot pelican. When a big tarpon flushes from such an apparition he makes a boil like a diving submarine. A bass may quietly sink and slide off under a stump, so we smugly continue to use heavier and shorter leaders than necessary. A bass striking a five-inch plug is so intent on the kill he probably doesn't notice twenty-pound line, but when sliding up to an imitation caddis or dragonfly he's apt to be more attentive.

Harry Murray, the Virginia bass and trout master, has written of smallmouth tactics that would be a new world to most long-term bass fishermen. Murray's stream moves are similar to what he would be using on educated trout and his constant success is proof of the whole business. For one thing, he goes into insect hatches that interest stream fish and sometimes fishes dry flies just as he would for trout. Few bass fishermen study hatches far enough to anticipate their dates on individual streams, but anyone not prepared to match a hatch of flies that bass are taking regularly just isn't trying hard enough.

I've encountered rises for everything from small caddisflies to burly cicadas on both lakes and streams. Frequently, such bass are on the prowl and will take almost anything that comes close to what they've been eating—but there are times when you need to match the hatch if you want to stay in the program with Harry Murray and his ilk. Usually, a hatch that appeals to bass will be matched by flies of #10 or larger, making it a little simpler than trout fishing, which might demand microscopic things with sadistically tiny hook eyes.

In current, most dry flies are fished in a "dead drift," imitating live insects with no control over their destinies, but in my experience bass will tolerate more extra motion in a fly than trout will, sometimes liking a few twitches. Twitches are nothing new to trout fishermen, of course, but most of the time the dry fly works better on trout when it floats dead on the water. Let's say the twitched bass fly is more likely to be successful.

The ideal way to fish a dry fly for bass is to cast it across and upstream and let it drift down until it begins to drag on the leader. If there's considerable current the bass will be facing upstream and we hope to show them the fly before they see the monofilament. Sometimes you'll have to cast straight upstream, thus showing your fish the leader or both leader and line as the fly drifts down; this is

Virginia smallmouth takes dead-drifted nymph in very shallow river water. The equipment is the same as used for trout.

not as neat as throwing up and across.

You can cast downstream and feed line to a drifting fly. I've had trouble setting a hook when fishing downstream but many experienced anglers swear by the method. When using the up-and-across cast, you can quickly learn to mend the line—flipping a loop of it above the fly before the thing starts to drag. Retrieve a little line and then let it go again and you get a little extra drift. The quick takeup that goes with that gets some strikes too. "Dragging" flies aren't as effective as twitched ones.

In stream fishing, nymphs take more study than anything that floats, simply because fishermen too often live in a dream world regarding what the things are doing down there. Spying on somebody else's nymphs from a bluff over clear water is disturbingly educational. Most bass nymphs are dead-drifted with a little manipulation now and then for best results.

Nymphs? Well maybe that's too dignified a name for things like Woolly Buggers and some of the wormlike horrors tied up by malevolent bass chasers. The time-honored routine is to cast upstream and across, mend the line a little, and let the lure swing down below the caster. Sinking tips, or even shooting heads, are almost a necessity in deeper water. A deliberately sloppy delivery with slack leader can be a help in getting a wet down to drift back under stumps or rocks. Casting nearly straight upstream with a slack leader can put a lure deep against a ledge that "faces" downstream.

So much bass fishing is done with a lure thrown near cover and pulled away from it that we sometimes forget the exact opposite can be effective. Some of my best fishing for largemouths involved casting from near the bank out across a bed of weeds and bringing a bug, streamer, or nymph back toward the cover. Almost anything a bass wants to eat is likely to seek refuge in cover rather than flee from it, and "pinning bait against the weeds" is an old bass stratagem. Harry Murray describes this in river fishing for smallmouths, wading into islands of grass and throwing out to their edges.

Bass, and especially smallmouths, are noted crayfish eaters and countless models of crayfish have been tied up from hair, feathers, and plastic. While most such imitations are impression-istic rather than attempts at exact duplication, it's wise to re-member how a real crayfish navigates, walking very slowly and swimming backward very swiftly. Things that don't look like crayfish at all may be taken by a fish looking for crayfish, if they are the right size and display the proper action.

Reading streams gets more complicated as a fisherman ad-vances, simply because he looks for things that didn't seem to be important at first.

Bass lying in fast water usually feed on station to some degree, covering only a small area and depending upon the current to bring food to them. A station is likely to be where some bottom charac-teristic causes an area in which the fish needs to fight the current less—behind or ahead of a boulder, for example, but where the fish can watch what comes along. In gently moving or dead water,

Drifting a nymph along a seam where a spring feeds into a smallmouth creek.

65

bass will cruise for their food and holding spots won't show so plainly.

"Seam" is a word hard-worked by experienced stream anglers. It means a place where two different currents or water forms join. Faster water joining slower water will make a visible seam as does current that has been divided by an obstacle, coming together again downstream. There is a seam at the edge of an eddy where currents are actually going in opposite directions. Bottom conformation can cause seams as current boils or speeds up.

The most plainly visible seams are where muddy or otherwise discolored water meets clearer water. A local rain can cause a feeder creek to run muddy while the main stream remains clear. Not only are bass likely to drop down from the feeder stream as it gets cloudy but there may be extra food where the mud comes in. The largest smallmouth I ever caught was waiting in clear water at the edge of such muddy current. The same thing can happen when the bigger stream is muddy and the feeder is clear.

Springs can cause an area of colder or warmer water, dependent upon the weather, and can be either above the surface or under it. Their seams may be invisible.

Most important of all, bass are to be found on the edges— edges of vegetation or "structure," edges of deeper, cooler, warmer, or clearer water, edges of shadow, and edges of various currents.

Good bass anglers are good watchers.

Along with Bass

6

There are no world-famous bluegill fishermen. A string of green sunfish will cause no dancing in the streets but water that contains bass almost invariably holds larger or smaller fish that takes flies. Most of them are "sunfish" and are thus close relatives of the black basses. Then there are the pikes, shad, and others, all considered warm-water fish, even though some of their water is a lot cooler than most bass prefer.

The truth is that fly rods catch more of these other fish than they do bass and it is a bit irritating to hear fishermen discussing me from a passing boat, saying it'd sure be funny to see that "brim fisherman" hook onto a bass and telling how a bass would break that fly pole. "Brim," incidentally, is a contraction of "bream," which usually means bluegill but often stands for anything smaller than bass, especially sunfish.

No one is counting but I believe the bluegill is the most popular of panfish for fly fishermen. It will strike on the surface, it grows large enough to be worthwhile as a table item, and it is said to be a harder fighter for its size than any bass that ever swam. I doubt the latter but can't prove it isn't so; I have also done a lot of rod bending on bluegills, firm in the belief that I had a pretty fair bass out there. Bluegills don't jump, but then neither do bluefin tuna.

My only complaint with the bluegill is that it comes with a pretty small mouth (as do some other sunfishes) and bluegill-catching efficiency demands a fly a little smaller than I'd like to use for bass. Much of the time I split the difference between a #10 for bluegills and a #2 for bass. I have not caught many good-sized largemouth bass on bluegill-sized bugs but I recall when my wife

67

cast a tiny rubber-legged "brim bug" against a raft of hyacinths and found that she and her little trout rod were attached to a 6½-pound bigmouth. For us at least, that was very unusual. I simply have not caught many good largemouth bass on #10 bugs. It would make a better story if they were real killers but if I wanted sizable largemouth bass I'd use at least a #6. Smallmouths like smaller lures, and we're generally satisfied with smaller bronzebacks anyhow. Anyway, a bass fisherman is equipped for bluegills with the addition of some smaller flies. If he gets serious he'll get a little rod.

Bugs used for bluegills should be fished slowly; in tests we've found that the very slowly worked sponge-rubber spider or small popping bug was more than 100 percent more effective when twitched only every ten seconds or so in competition with the same bug twitched every second. Of course there are times when this might not be true but I'm convinced that the slow and gentle bug will beat the quick and noisy one most of the time. Although bluegills will often strike big bass bugs, they generally do it when the big ones aren't worked very fast and often you won't hook their small mouths.

I have no preference for bug color although I guess I've used yellow and green ones more than anything else. I have found that rubber legs or loosely waving feather strands add to a bug's attraction for bluegills. For that matter, as stated elsewhere, they have increased the effectiveness of bass bugs too.

Wet or dry trout flies will catch plenty of bluegills and similar panfish. With small flies, however, we have a problem of small, greedy fish either swallowing them or getting them so far down that a major operation is necessary in hook removal. The bluegill's tiny mouth (same as with some other panfish) doesn't accept fingers and isn't even easy for needle-nosed pliers. A tiny trout fly is an executioner and you'll have some troubles even with a #10.

Bluegills are good evening feeders, and in warm weather they seem to come on right at dusk. I have found on some lakes that they become receptive somewhat later than the bass do. When they're ready for surface bugs or flies you can generally hear them along the edges of cover.

"Bumblebee" bug with rubber legs took this 8½-pounder
for Ray Donnersberger.

For fish so easily caught, they can be pretty tricky at times, especially regarding water depth. There are days when they simply won't come up very far for a fly but will take with enthusiasm when it is delivered at the proper depth. At other times they insist on something on top. I don't offer scientific solutions but I do want to encourage some experimentation. Some instances:

On a slow-moving California river I saw a minor disturbance in a little backwater, diagnosed it as bluegills feeding, and confidently tied on a little wet fly. The water was only a few inches deep. I couldn't raise a fish although they kept moving and I began to think they weren't bluegills at all. Then, my wet fly floated briefly before going down—and a bluegill grabbed it. I then doped the fly so it would float and caught a bunch of them. When it sank it had been only inches down but they'd have none of it. In that case I think a small bug or rubber spider would have been better than a true dry fly. It was the shallowest water I have ever fished for bluegills and the larger ones kept showing their backs as they fed—but I don't think they were taking anything from the surface except my fly. Live and learn?

I once got into a bass and panfish fly-fishing contest, my first and last experience in competition fishing. I got into it by accident but couldn't back out when the chips were down. We were releasing the fish so it could have been worse. Anyway, on one day of the contest I had to catch a limit of panfish before I could turn to the business of chasing bass, which were found for the most part in other areas. The object was to catch all those bluegills in a hurry and for the first time I felt pressure in bluegill fishing. I had a guide who knew his way around.

The bluegills were in a deep Florida canal and it was the peak of their spawning period. As the boat slid along under oars we could make out light spots on the bottom near shore and we knew they were bluegill beds. Now and then I could actually see a fish moving, several feet down, and with the confidence of a closed mind I began working the area with small bugs. Now and then I caught a fish. If they'd come up for the bug, I reasoned, there was no use in trying anything else. My guide fidgeted.

"Don't you think we ought to hurry up and get this bluegill

Bluegills have a strong preference for slow-moving bugs with rubber legs and come in colors to match their habitat. This large and nearly black one came from vegetation blackened water.

limit over with?'' he asked.

This effrontery toward a panfish wizard like me was unheard of but I treated him with kindly tolerance and asked if he had any suggestions. He said he had tied some nymphs that would catch bluegills as fast as I could cast and count.

The nymphs were much like Woolly Worms, dark green with little feather tails. They were slightly weighted. I condescendingly tied one on and flipped it over an area of beds. He explained that I had to get it down to the exact level (floating line but fairly long leader) and the best way was to count as it went down. He made a good guess at the depth on the first cast and thirty-two half-pound bluegills later we went bass fishing. More than half of my casts had resulted in strikes.

It isn't always that good but getting to the correct depth is much of the battle. The deceiving part is that a few fish will change depth considerably as they had done for my bug and, like me, you might miss the really good fishing. Complacency is relaxing—but it doesn't catch the most fish.

I believe the nymph is the most deadly of fly-rod attractions for panfish as a group, year in and year out. I have had most success with dark colors and prefer dark green although black or brown will do well too. I've caught most of the panfish with nymphs, including green sunfish, pumpkinseed sunfish, white and yellow perch, and so on. The shellcracker (red-eared sunfish) isn't noted as a fly-taker but I've done very well on them with weighted nymphs. For what it's worth, I have used bigger nymphs for shellcrackers and they often enough take bass, a happy premium in most panfish waters.

It takes an entire book to break down all of the panfish names, local and scientific, identical names used for different fish in different localities, making me feel that there may be some merit in lumping them all off as "bream," as they do in the South. However, some of them have such distinctive characteristics they must be treated separately.

The green sunfish doesn't get very large but it has a big mouth and is noted for banging big bass bugs. I have waded a lot of miles of midwestern creeks, telling myself I was primarily after bass but catching a dozen green sunfish for every largemouth. In most cases, the usual bass manipulation works fine on green sunfish (when I first caught them we called them "black perch"). The rock bass will take medium-sized bass bugs too and has saved the day for me on some Ozark streams when the smallmouths were uncooperative. Rock bass are called "goggle-eye" there. Farther south, the warmouth has a similiar mouth and is a very close relative, but it doesn't seem to get as big as the rock bass.

I have caught a great many white perch on small streamers and bugs cast for bass and can recall a day on one of Maine's granite lakes when the perch came from very shallow water and took everything in the box. When a smallmouth finally did come booming up from sunken boulders it's a wonder I didn't break him off in near-apoplexy. The yellow perch is less of a surface striker in my experience but can be had with tiny streamers and deep wets.

Crappie will take surface lures but my first choice for them would be weighted nymphs and I've done my best with sinking-tip lines. There are, of course, times when crappie are pretty deep for practical fly fishing but diehard disciples can do a good job on them. One thing that works is a tiny jig, tied wet—that is, it uses a jig hook but with somewhat less weight than would be used on a spinning rod. Especially around brush piles or drowned treetops, crappie like a lure that lifts gently and then settles toward the bottom. You can come close to this action with a little streamer of normal shape but the lopsided mounting afforded by the little jig hook makes it work easier. My recommendation is to work crappie lures as slow as possible—and then a little slower. A little glitter adds to crappie flies, easily provided by the commercial Mylar products in very small strands. For that matter, the shiny stuff adds appeal to most bass and panfish attractors. I lose a lot of flies when I "jig" them for crappies, making short casts over brushy cover. They can be weedless to some extent but stiff weed-guards don't work well with gentle takes.

In preparation for spawning, crappies sometimes become easy marks along shallow shorelines, but the calendar is only partly reliable and many crappie have changed that program from year to year. Like many other panfish they hold in loose schools, frequently making my fishing feast or famine. The prospecting part can be time consuming.

The chain pickerel, smaller cousin of the northern pike and muskellunge, takes near-surface streamers well in weedy waters. Although I've caught them on popping bugs, my first choice is a rather fast-moving streamer with lots of flash, and if you really go in after them a weed-guard is a help. They do considerable following, making slashing false strikes as they come. Generally, when fishing for bass and an assortment of panfish, I can tell immediately if a pickerel is in the mood. In fishing near the surface, I just speed it up and keep it coming. If I'm fishing deep, I forget the hurry part—a fine distinction, but the chances are I won't know I have a following pickerel if the fly is very far down there. In pure pickerel fishing you'll want a bit of heavy tippet material or some light wire

Chain pickerel are often found in the same water as bass and will take the same lures although they generally prefer a faster-moving streamer.

in deference to sharp teeth. Pickerel will often strike just as you lift a fly from the water, so fish your fly carefully until the last moment.

Northern pike deserve a better reputation as fly takers; they crunch balsa bugs and bite off leaders. I like to work big streamers and bugs pretty fast for them and I think glitter is even more important than for bass. A heavy monofilament shock tippet will work although I've also used wire. When I'm really after northerns I like at least a #8 rod, not only because I need to keep them out of weeds but because the flies and bugs are pretty big. I have never found it necessary to use light leaders for them. I think any good-sized bass lure will work for pike and adding speed and glitter helps most of the time.

Northern pike will take most of the lures used for bass and are not
particular about leaders. Light wire or heavy monofilament shock tippets
are called for.

Boats and Boots

Bass have been caught from everything from yachts to inner tubes. The modern bass boat is a marvel of efficiency for the bigger bass waters and its electronic gear is a help for any fisherman.

The modern electric motor has virtually replaced pole, paddle, and oars for bass on big water. I have fished with it in water so shallow it dug mud and modern propellers pull it through a surprising stand of weeds without trouble.

Does it scare fish? It sure does sometimes, but so does a white shirt. If an electric motor is running in shallow water you should keep your casts fairly long, for even a bass that shows no sign of fright may have no intention of striking as long as he hears the strange noise—and the most quiet electric motor sends sound under water. Starting and stopping an electric scares fish more than letting it run steadily.

Foot-controlled electrics provide one more thing to tangle in fly lines and nearly all of us coil line on the deck at least part of the time. Most foot controls are hard to operate unless you're sitting down. Bass-boat seats are fine and nearly all casters can operate from a chair. "Leaning post" installations are good, especially in rough water, but most bass fishing is done where there isn't much bounce.

Conventional high-speed bass boats generally lack good storage area for the long rods. In seeking the best, purely for fly-rod fishing, the flats boats that are used for bonefish can be just as fast as the bass boats, are likely to be a bit more seaworthy and are likely to have good rod storage. They have higher freeboard, making them less maneuverable with the electric motor in wind.

Electric motor works for fly caster using bottom-bumping nymph in offshore water of impoundment.

Multi-purpose boat designed mainly for use on salt-water flats serves for bass and panfish in a deep drainage canal.

The electronic fishfinders of bass boats are most helpful on big lakes, especially impoundments; they help the deep-water lure or bait fisherman far more than the fly fisher. Water thermometers are a help when you're looking for cooler or warmer water.

The johnboat, flat-bottomed and generally made of aluminum, is about as practical as you can get in a light outboard craft. I have been especially pleased with a fourteen-footer using a 25-horse motor; it's easily launched and retrieved, and fast enough for most waters. Aluminum is noisy, however, even in a light chop, and with no chop at all it's easy to spread an alarm with feet or equipment.

The more ornate aluminum fishing boats generally have carpeting to deaden noise from the occupants but few johnboats come that way. We have used outdoor carpeting on ours; I've had a lot of them, the first ones used as cartoppers. When the car manufac-

turers made cartopping difficult, I started using light trailers and my johnboats got bigger. Fourteen feet is a handy size and a sixteen-footer isn't too big for most small waters. Johnboats aren't perfect and the flat bottom is difficult to winch onto a trailer unless everything is exactly right. I use both oars and electric motors with them. Unless they're carefully fitted, the oars are noisier than the electric motor.

Inflated boats are quiet, easily transported, and efficient in small waters. The wind can make them hard to handle but I've gone a lot of miles in them. A close relative is the "belly boat" or "floater bubble," available with all sorts of storage and creature comforts. In support of recent articles revealing they have been

Fully equipped largemouth bass fisherman with waders, boat, and "floater bubble."

Fourteen-foot johnboat with medium-sized gasoline outboard and an electric motor is an easily transported and handled rig for fly fishing.

around for "ten years or more," I can recall their use for more than half a century. They're wonderful in deep canals unsuited to "real" boats.

Canoes can be silent and topnotch for drifting many bass rivers. They, too, work fine on canals and small lakes. Unfortunately for some areas, canoes are so much fun that bass rivers can be crowded by nonfishing canoeists likely to pull alongside a wading angler to watch him play the biggest bass he's seen all year.

Anyone doing much wading for bass in cool water should have chest waders. There is an old adage that the chief advantage of hip boots is that they hold more water than knee boots. Insulation is seldom needed in most bass water. There are a few swift smallmouth streams where aluminum cleats are a help on algae-slick rocks but you can generally get by with felt soles, and ordinary rubber soles are fine for nearly all lake fishing. Some of the toughest heavy-duty rubber waders are black and they can be much hotter than tan ones. In bass fishing, waders are more likely to be too warm than too cold and insulated ones are seldom needed.

Having fly-fished for bass from almost any kind of boat that floats (and a couple that sank) I become more and more insistent on silent progress. I am convinced that the steady buzz of an electric motor is better than the occasional thump of somebody moving a cooler or stumbling over an anchor. I am also convinced there is no sound better than silence for I have watched too many waders outfish boaters beside them. This is especially true in fly fishing, which, despite our methods of deep fishing, is usually carried on in shallow water. Sloppy wading can scare fish, however, and when sloshing through tightly woven vegetation it's possible to shake up a bass fifty feet away. Still, as long as you don't shake the landscape or make noise, bass can be caught very close to a pair of waders.

I have known excellent bass water to be ruined by fast boat traffic that continually washed the shorelines. On the other hand, fish that are used to boats are easier to approach and settle down quicker after being disturbed. That's the way they live. And many a resort lake that is churned by speedboats and water skiers during the day can be especially good fishing at dawn and at night. If they don't feed during the day they'll be hungrier at other times.

The spookiest bass of all are likely to be in water that sees no boats or waders. I proved this to myself when I was doing well from canal banks and launched a small boat to really cover the area. The boat often puts the fish on the run in narrow ditches, even when carefully operated—and although a wake dies quickly, some fish seem to have good memories.

Wet wading works in the summertime and this caster keeps all of his flies atop his head.

An Endless Supply?

8

There are more black bass now than ever before. Their ranges have been expanded by human activities. At the same time, some treasured forms of fly fishing for bass have deteriorated.

The great impoundments provide millions more black bass than were present before they were built. However, many of our finest bass streams have disappeared as the dams went in. That's been especially hard on drift-boating and fly fishing on famous smallmouth rivers of another era. Of course it is possible that many of those streams wouldn't have withstood the pressure of today's population anyway. A few are left. There is fly fishing on most of the impoundments, a somewhat different sport from river angling. Generally speaking, the largemouth holds forth strongly in impoundments, whereas it might not have been present in the rivers before they were dammed. Impoundments are the backbone of modern technical bass-boat fishing, a science of awesome proportions despite its image of speedboats, competition, and backwoods rhetoric.

Bass management has changed constantly, fisheries biologists frequently having to unsell the public from yesterday's outmoded programs. Although hatcheries are needed occasionally when fish are introduced to brand-new waters or when some disaster wipes out a population, the "plant and harvest" policy is virtually dead. Proper habitat and controlled catches are the major factors.

Bass fishing boomed with the colorful entrance of bass tournaments and their exotic equipment. The rage for bass fishing ensured that bass management would be a major project of state conservation agencies; but at the same time, added pressure on the resource began to discredit a policy of recent years. Simply stated, the policy had been that hook-and-line fishing with liberal limits could not damage a bass population. It was hard-sold to the public in discrediting outdated cries for more bass hatcheries.

Then it developed that while heavy fishing pressure could not destroy a bass population it became clear that fish in the desirable sizes could become very scarce. A system of "slot limits" has proved effective in some hard-pressed areas—that is, although trophy bass are kept, "medium-sized" bass, making up most of the desirable catch, must be released. This does not mean that there is a dearth of tiny bass since one female could populate a good-sized lake if her hatch escaped predation.

Although fly fishing has not made much of a splash in big-time bass tournaments, the tournament people have helped in preaching catch-and-release and promoting other conservation practices. The

Canal fisherman proves neither big water nor big boats are necessary for big bass. You can have lots of fun with bass in humble places.

black basses have an excellent survival rate when released, actually surviving rather crude handling in most cases. The catch-and-release movement is growing but the bass fishermen are still well behind trout anglers at that.

One recent management innovation is a winner on easily controlled impoundments. The "draw-down" involves lowering the water level drastically, exposing additional shoreline to the sun, thus giving the effect of a new impoundment when the water rises again. This has been working for only a few years on the most adaptable lakes and there may be a limit as to how many times it can be used in a given location. The procedure must be repeated at intervals and not every resort owner is happy to have his pier left high and dry, even temporarily.

Pollution can sometimes be temporarily blocked by the drawdown, but in other waters, where sewage and agricultural or industrial chemicals are the culprits, there are no easy solutions and bass fishing has been eliminated in a few cases and badly damaged in others.

During the period when it was constantly preached that hook and line could not harm bass populations, we did away with closed seasons in many parts of the country. Formerly, the closed season was primarily to protect fish during the spawning season. Then it was concluded by biologists that only a tiny percentage of the bass hatch could be accommodated and that the loss of spawning fish had no effect on the overall population. This has never been disproved but there is a different bugaboo that goes with fishing over spawning fish. The fact is that the largest fish are likely to be spawners and the least likely to be released by anglers. And "fishing the beds" can be a deadly method when practiced by experts.

There are some lakes in the South where anglers rig high vantage points on their boats and are able to sight the light-colored bass beds with big females on them. They then use live bait, repeatedly throwing a minnow into the nest. It takes a long time to develop a big female bass and when water conditions are just right (or wrong) most of them can be caught, especially if expert guides are seeking trophies for their clients. I have watched this happen in two areas when a year of big fish was followed by a season in which

The "drawdown" has proved a successful operation on impounded lakes. Low water exposes shallow shorelines to sunlight and bass habitat improves with a return to higher levels.

the guides swore the fishing had gone to hell. The overall population wasn't damaged but the big ones were gone and the taxidermists suffered.

Of course there are horror stories of illegal bass fishing, some of them true, but most violations of the rules are minor. There are commercial fishermen for other species who do not release bass caught in nets. There have been some instances when expert cast-netters captured spawning fish from the beds. When bass fishing is especially good there are a few fishermen who take one limit home and are back to fishing again on the same day. Most of these violations have only minor effect.

Where legal, fly fishermen operate during spawning season the same as everyone else. Before and after spawning, bass are especially hungry but I believe no harm is done. I do believe the use of live bait over sighted beds is bad news—but overall closing during spawning is not practical in most cases. Closing spawning areas while other fishing continues was once classified as pure public relations by fisheries biologists. Right now they are not so sure, and if there are benefits they are hard to total. I do know that some closed areas have been especially good fishing when the ban was lifted after the main spawning season had ended.

Overpopulation by panfish, especially bluegills, can actually harm the bass population in some cases. Bluegills are eager feeders on bass eggs. And where bluegills are overcrowded they become stunted and aren't valuable as fishing targets themselves.

A final thought: fly fishing, where the emphasis is on *how* you fish, not how many fish you catch, and where a single hook is the rule (and this can be de-barbed), encourages the conservation of the bass resource. There isn't an endless supply of any gamefish these days; the pleasure of fly-rodding for bass can help preserve what there is.

Brief Bibliography

BERGMAN, Ray. *Fresh-Water Bass*

LIVINGSTON, A. D. *Fly-Rodding for Bass*

McNALLY, Tom. *Fly Fishing*

MURRAY, Harry. *Fly Fishing for Smallmouth Bass*

SOSIN, Mark, and Bill Dance. *Practical Black Bass Fishing*

WATERMAN, Charles F. *Modern Fresh and Salt Water Fly Fishing*

WHITLOCK, Dave. *L. L. Bean Fly Fishing for Bass Handbook*